ON CITY STREETS

An Anthology of Poetry

SELECTED BY NANCY LARRICK

Illustrated with photographs by David Sagarin

M. Evans and Company, Inc.
NEW YORK

M. Evans and Company, Inc.
216 East 49 Street
New York, New York 10017

Thanks are due to the following authors, publishers, publications and agents for permission to use the material included:

Antioch Review for "On Watching The Construction Of A Skyscraper" by Burton Raffel, copyright 1960 by the Antioch Press.

Atheneum House, Inc. for "Construction," "Joralemon Street," "The Streetcleaner's Lament" and "Ten O'Clock." Copyright © 1965 by Patricia Hubbell, from 8 A.M. SHADOWS. Used by permission of Atheneum Publishers; "A Lazy Thought." Copyright © 1962 by Eve Merriam, from THERE IS NO RHYME FOR SILVER. Used by permission of Atheneum Publishers; "City Traffic." Copyright © 1964 by Eve Merriam, from IT DOESN'T ALWAYS HAVE TO RHYME. Used by permission of Atheneum Publishers; "Alligator on the Escalator." Copyright © 1966 by Eve Merriam, from CATCH A LITTLE RHYME. Used by permission of Atheneum Publishers.

ACKNOWLEDGMENTS

On City Streets has been compiled with the help of more than one hundred inner-city and small-city youngsters—too many to list as several urgently requested, but all deeply appreciated. Their interest in the search for poetry about the city and their perceptive comments about which poems should be included in this anthology made me realize more strongly than ever that children have a natural flair for poetry and a critical sense that adults should heed. To these poetry critics, I am warmly grateful.

Among the adults who have assisted in the search for city poems and who have read and commented on proposed selections, I wish to thank Fred Schalow of the Graduate School of Library Science, Drexel Institute; Isabel Heller and her colleagues of the Philadelphia Public Schools; Joanne Horvath and Viola Long, teachers in Bethlehem, Pennsylvania; Phoebe Crosby, Elsa Ueland and Betty Bettman of Flourtown, Pennsylvania; and—most important—my husband Alexander L. Crosby, who read, listened, criticized and encouraged along the way.

NANCY LARRICK

ON CITY STREETS

As a fifteen-year-old, I moved from the easy-going beauty of a country town into the clatter of a great city. Baltimore's downtown streets were dirty. The scanty trees were stunted. Sidewalks were often cluttered with the overflow from unemptied trash cans. Streetcars whined to a halt outside my window as they picked up passengers.

But I loved it. I spent hours poking around the old Lexington Market, exploring the Baltimore waterfront, and riding the open-top Charles Street buses. There was an excitement about all of this which is more vivid to me now than any college lecture or discussion I can recall.

When I headed to New York for a year of graduate study, I took the train to Jersey City and then the ferry to Manhattan for that unforgettable view of the downtown skycrapers. "The city spreads its wings," wrote Langston Hughes. And here it was before me.

But even at a great city university where students were almost intoxicated by the city's rhythm, we met no city poetry. To enjoy Wordsworth's "host of golden daffodils," I had to shut out the sights and sounds of Broadway and go back to the country roads I had explored as a child in the Shenandoah Valley. A nice nostalgic exercise—and for me a pleasant one, but it never did for me what the subways and skyscrapers of New York were doing day and night.

Then—almost accidentally—I met the poetry of Walt Whitman, the Brooklyn printer who wrote and set in type *Leaves of Grass* in 1855. Could this be poetry? Nurtured as I had been on "the modest violet," I could hardly believe that a poet would say,

> *Give me such shows—give me the streets of*
> *Manhattan!*
> *Give me Broadway. . . .*

Here was someone who had found miracles in the streets, who had written with boiling compulsion about the Brooklyn ferry, city pavements and row houses, the shops and shows, the people on crowded streets. It seemed impossible!

And in Whitman's day it *was* impossible for this to be called poetry by more than a tiny circle. Recognition came slowly, but *Leaves of Grass* has now been translated into most of the languages of the world, and Walt Whitman is honored as one of the great voices of America.

Nevertheless, the tradition of rural poetry prevailed in America for years. Carl Sandburg's *Chicago* in 1916 and *Smoke and Steel* in 1920 were among the first books to break the pattern. A few years later, Langston Hughes wrote about New York City as he had seen it from a Harlem tenement. By 1968 the most vibrant poetry in America sings of urban people, their passions and their problems.

What about poetry for young people? For many years children's poets wrote only sweet gentle songs of country life. Anthologists, compiling for young readers, selected poems about fragrant hay and pumpkin vines. These seemed more fitting for youngsters in a rural society.

But today most Americans live in the city, and even those in small towns and rural areas are just as urbanized as their city cousins, thanks to television. Rural children in a school bus can tell you more about the bus and the traffic lights than flowers along their country road. City children who sit silent in class become voluble when given a chance to talk or write about their world of city streets.

On City Streets is a collection of poems about city sights and city people. The poems have been selected with the help of more than one hundred young readers in inner-city and small-city schools. Not every poem is liked equally well, of course, but each one is included because of strong advocates among the young.

Many of the poems in this collection tell of the bitter tragedies of city life. "Mother to Son" by Langston Hughes, "The Sad Story About Greenwich Village" by Frances Park, and "Taught Me Purple" by Evelyn Tooley Hunt were favorites in every inner-city classroom I visited. Even young suburbanites recommended these poems, saying, "We ought to know about these things. They're real."

I was happy to find that those who insisted on

poems that are "real" also welcomed the fantastic nonsense of Eve Merriam's "Alligator on the Escalator" and John Holmes's "Rhyme of Rain."

On City Streets, then, is made up of young people's choices—poems sometimes nonsensical, more often tinged with tragedy, but always vibrant with the drama of city life today.

NANCY LARRICK

March 29, 1968

CONTENTS

Roaring, Clanking,
Sirens Screaming

BROADWAY: TWILIGHT

Roaring, clanking,
Sirens screaming
In confusion;
Pink and yellow,
Shifting, gleaming
In profusion.

Above the deepening blue
The stars blink calmly through.

TOM PRIDEAUX

CITY TRAFFIC

Green as a seedling the one lane shines,
Red ripened blooms for the opposite lines;
Emerald shoot,
Vermilion fruit.

Now amber, now champagne, now honey: go slow:
Shift, settle, then gather and sow.

EVE MERRIAM

JORALEMON STREET

We walked in the sun on Joralemon Street.
(Geraniums white and geraniums pink
Brightened the flats on Joralemon Street.)
The sun rode the brownstones
A short pace away.
And turned before settling night on the day
To wave us a shadow that banded the street.
(Geranium guarded Joralemon Street.)
He slid from the housetops
And hurried away
Leaving night in his place on the husk of the day,
And we walked in the shadows along the dark street
And knew how geraniums smell in the dusk.

PATRICIA HUBBELL

CITY TREES

The trees along this city street,
    Save for the traffic and the trains,
Would make a sound as thin and sweet
    As trees in country lanes.

And people standing in their shade
    Out of a shower, undoubtedly
Would hear such music as is made
    Upon a country tree.

Oh, little leaves that are so dumb
    Against the shrieking city air,
I watch you when the wind has come,—
    I know what sound is there.

EDNA ST. VINCENT MILLAY

THE TERM

A rumpled sheet
of brown paper
about the length

and apparent bulk
of a man was
rolling with the

wind slowly over
and over in
the street as

a car drove down
upon it and
crushed it to

the ground. Unlike
a man it rose
again rolling

with the wind over
and over to be as
it was before.

WILLIAM CARLOS WILLIAMS

In the street I have just left
the small leaves of the trees along the gutter
were steadfast
in the blue heavens.
Now the subway
express
picks up speed
and a wind
blows through the car,
blows dust
on the passengers,
and along the floor
bits of paper—
wrappers of candy,
of gum, tinfoil,
pieces of newspaper. . .

CHARLES REZNIKOFF

THE STREETCLEANER'S LAMENT

dirt and
clean them clean them clean them
dirt and
leave them let them rot
dirt and stench and
clean them clean them
bending at the waist and stabbing—
papers papers blowing sticking
never leave them
clean them clean them
people put them
now remove them
clean streets sidewalks
quick
remove them
dirt and dirt and dirt forever.

PATRICIA HUBBELL

DOG AROUND THE BLOCK

Dog around the block, sniff,
Hydrant sniffing, corner, grating,
Sniffing, always, starting forward,
Backward, dragging, sniffing backward,
Leash at taut, leash at dangle,
Leash in people's feet entangle—
Sniffing dog, apprised of smellings,
Meeting enemies,
Loving old acquaintances, sniff,
Sniffing hydrant for reminders,
Leg against the wall, raise,
Leaving grating, corner greeting,
Chance for meeting, sniff, meeting,
Meeting, telling, news of smelling,
Nose to tail, tail to nose,
Rigid, careful, pose,
Liking, partly liking, hating,
Then another hydrant, grating,
Leash at taut, leash at dangle,
Tangle, sniff, untangle,
Dog around the block, sniff.

E. B. WHITE

The wind blows the rain into our faces
as we go down the hillside
upon rusted cans and old newspapers,
past the tree on whose bare branches
the boys have hung iron hoops,
until we reach at last the crushed earthworms
stretched and stretching on the wet sidewalk.

CHARLES REZNIKOFF

RHYME OF RAIN

"Fifty stories more to fall,
Nothing in our way at all,"
Said a raindrop to its mate,
Falling near the Empire State.
Said the second, "Here we go!
That's Fifth Avenue below."
Said the first one, "There's a hat.
Watch me land myself on that.
Forty stories isn't far—
Thirty seven—here we are—
Twenty, sixteen, thirteen, ten—"
"If we make this trip again,"
Said the second, "we must fall
Near a building twice as tall."
"What a time to think of that,"
Said the first, and missed the hat.

JOHN HOLMES

Q IS FOR THE QUIETNESS

Q is for the Quietness
    Of Sunday avenues
When silence walks the city
    In her pretty velvet shoes;
When trucks forget to rumble,
    And from steeples everywhere
The bells of Sunday morning
    Ring their questions on the air.

PHYLLIS McGINLEY

SUNDAY

This is the day when all through the town
the cats are keeping store,
the clerks are gone from counter and desk,
the key has turned in the door.

But the cats move about with an owner's airs
over the oranges, apples, and pears,

or among the tins in their rows on the shelves,
proud as merchants and nimble as elves.

Then at last they each lie down to rest
where the big show window is sunniest,

or turn to stare at the passer-by
with a calculating but sleepy eye.

In every one of the forty-eight states,
in a thousand cities or more,
from Saturday night to Monday at seven
the cats are keeping store!

ELIZABETH COATSWORTH

CITY AUTUMN

The air breathes frost. A thin wind beats
Old dust and papers down gray streets
And blows brown leaves with curled-up edges
At frightened sparrows on window ledges.
A snow-flake falls like an errant feather:
A vagabond draws his cloak together,
And an old man totters past with a cane
Wondering if he'll see Spring again.

JOSEPH MONCURE MARCH

A PATCH OF OLD SNOW

There's a patch of old snow in a corner
    That I should have guessed
Was a blow-away paper the rain
    Had brought to rest.

It is speckled with grime as if
    Small print overspread it,
The news of a day I've forgotten—
    If I ever read it.

ROBERT FROST

RIVER NIGHT

Up and down the river
The barges go:
Whether moons are yellow,
Whether stars flow
Softly over city,
Softly over town,
Sleepily the barges
Go up and down.

Up and down the river
On summer nights
The barges drift,
And emerald lights
And crimson prick
The darkness under
Blown-out stars
And gathering thunder.

Up and down the river
The barges go,
Up and down the darkness
River-winds blow,
And sleepers in a city
And sleepers in a town
Dream of the barges
Going up and down.

FRANCES FROST

WATER-FRONT STREETS

The spring is not so beautiful there—
    But dream ships sail away
To where the spring is wondrous rare
    And life is gay.

The spring is not so beautiful there—
    But lads put out to sea
Who carry beauties in their hearts
    And dreams, like me.

LANGSTON HUGHES

THE MOUTH OF THE HUDSON

A single man stands like a bird-watcher,
and scuffles the pepper and salt snow
from a discarded, gray
Westinghouse Electric cable drum.
He cannot discover America by counting
the chains of condemned freight-trains
from thirty states. They jolt and jar
and junk in the siding below him.
He has trouble with his balance.
His eyes drop,
and he drifts with the wild ice
ticking seaward down the Hudson,
like the blank sides of a jig-saw puzzle.

The ice ticks seaward like a clock.
A Negro toasts
wheat-seeds over the coke-fumes
in a punctured barrel.
Chemical air
sweeps in from New Jersey
and smells of coffee.
Across the river,
ledges of suburban factories tan
in the sulfur-yellow sun
of the unforgivable landscape.

ROBERT LOWELL

Tall People,
Short People

PEOPLE

Tall people, short people,
Thin people, fat,
Lady so dainty
Wearing a hat,
Straight people, dumpy people,
Man dressed in brown;
Baby in a buggy—
These make a town.

LOIS LENSKI

A LAZY THOUGHT

There go the grownups
To the office,
To the store.
Subway rush,
Traffic crush;
Hurry, scurry,
Worry, flurry.

No wonder
Grownups
Don't grow up
Any more.

It takes a lot
Of slow
To grow.

EVE MERRIAM

ALLIGATOR ON THE ESCALATOR

Through the revolving door
Of a department store
There slithered an alligator.

When he came to the escalator,
He stepped upon the track with great dexterity;
His tail draped over the railing,
And he clicked his teeth in glee:
    "Yo, I'm off on the escalator,
    Excited as I can be!
    It's a *moving* experience,
    As you can plainly see.
    On the moving stair I go anywhere,
    I rise to the top
    Past outerwear, innerwear,
    Dinnerwear, thinnerwear—
    Then down to the basement with bargains galore,
    Then back on the track to the top once more!
    Oh, I may ride the escalator
    Until closing time or later,
    So tell the telephone operator
    To call Mrs. Albert Q. Alligator
    And tell her to take a hot mud bath
    And not to wait up for me!"

EVE MERRIAM

EMMA'S STORE

The store we like best is Emma's store.
It hasn't any revolving door.

It hasn't a floorman neat and polite:
"Third floor, Modom, and turn to your right."

No elevators go up and down it.
Nothing's the way it is downtown. It

Hasn't a special place for dresses;
Everything's jumbled in cozy messes—

Washcloths and lamp shades, paper dolls, slippers,
Candy and shoestrings, umbrellas and zippers;

No matter what's needed or how great the hurry
As long as there's Emma's, you don't need to worry,

And *she* never minds how long you stay.
"Why sure, take your time, dear," Emma will say.

DOROTHY ALDIS

PEOPLE WHO MUST

I painted on the roof of a skyscraper.
I painted a long while and called it a day's work.
The people on a corner swarmed and the traffic cop's
     whistle never let up all afternoon.
They were the same as bugs, many bugs on
     their way—
Those people on the go or at a standstill;
And the traffic cop a spot of blue, a splinter of brass,
Where the black tides ran around him
And he kept the street. I painted a long while
And called it a day's work.

CARL SANDBURG

PROLETARIAN PORTRAIT

A big young bareheaded woman
in an apron

Her hair slicked back standing
on the street

One stockinged foot toeing
the sidewalk

Her shoe in her hand. Looking
intently into it

She pulls out the paper insole
to find the nail

That has been hurting her.

WILLIAM CARLOS WILLIAMS

STREET WINDOW

The pawn-shop man knows hunger,
And how far hunger has eaten the heart
Of one who comes with an old keepsake.
Here are wedding rings and baby bracelets,
Scarf pins and shoe buckles, jeweled garters,
Old-fashioned knives with inlaid handles,
Watches of old gold and silver,
Old coins worn with finger-marks.
They tell stories.

CARL SANDBURG

THE FLOWER-CART MAN

When it's just past April
    And going on May,
The bent old Flower Man
    Comes our way.

His clothes are very baggy,
    His horse is lean and gray.
But, like a walking garden,
    His cart with plants is gay.

All filled with nodding rose trees
    To make your parlor bright,
With tulips for your table,
    Or daisies gold and bright.

With pansy plants and lilies,
    Primrose and daffodil,
And red geraniums in pots
    To trim your window sill.

Everywhere his cart goes
    The air smells sweet,
As the gray horse and he
    Jog from street to street.

They say that Spring's a lady
    And it may be so,
Though she never stopped on our street
    As far as I know—

But the bent old Flower Man
    Comes our way,
When it's just past April
    And going on May.

RACHEL FIELD

COBBLER

He mends the shoes
and watches the feet
of the crowd that goes
along the street.

A basement deep
and a sidewalk high;
along the ceiling
the feet go by;

toeing and heeling
they seem to skim
the top of the larky ·
world to him

in the dusty dark,
whose eyes dilate
as he gazes up
through the dingy grate.

The world hobbles
on feet of clay,
the cobbler cobbles
his days away;

crooked heels
and broken toes
are all he feels,
all he knows.

PEGGY BACON

YOUNG WOMAN
AT A WINDOW

She sits with
tears on

her cheek
her cheek on

her hand
the child

in her lap
his nose

pressed
to the glass

WILLIAM CARLOS WILLIAMS

BIRTHPLACE REVISITED

I stand in the dark light in the dark street
and look up at my window, I was born there.
The lights are on; other people are moving about.
I am with raincoat; cigarette in mouth,
hat over eye, hand on gat.
I cross the street and enter the building.
The garbage cans haven't stopped smelling.
I walk up the first flight; Dirty Ears
aims a knife at me . . .
I pump him full of lost watches.

GREGORY CORSO

WE REAL COOL

The Pool Players.
Seven at the Golden Shovel.

We real cool. We
Left school. We

Lurk late. We
Strike straight. We

Sing sin. We
Thin gin. We

Jazz June. We
Die soon.

GWENDOLYN BROOKS

MANHATTAN EPITAPHS: LAWYER

He sent so many
to jail for life,
so many
to sudden death,
he finally lost
his own private case
because he was out of
breath.

ALFRED KREYMBORG

COMMUTER

Commuter—one who spends his life
In riding to and from his wife;
A man who shaves and takes a train
And then rides back to shave again.

E. B. WHITE

FATIGUE

The man in the corner
all slumped over
looks forlorner
than a tired lover,

forehead dulled
with heavy working,
eyelids lulled
by the train's jerking;

head hangs noddy,
limbs go limply,
among a number
he dozes simply;

a dumb slumber,
a dead ending,
a spent body
homeward wending.

PEGGY BACON

SUBWAY RUSH HOUR

Mingled
breath and smell
so close
mingled
black and white
so near
no room for fear.

LANGSTON HUGHES

HUSBANDS AND WIVES

Husbands and wives
    With children between them
Sit in the subway;
    So I have seen them.

One word only
    From station to station;
So much talk for
    So close a relation.

MIRIAM HERSHENSON

MIDNIGHT RAFFLE

I put my nickel
In the raffle in the night.
Somehow that raffle
Didn't turn out right.

I lost my nickle.
I lost my time.
I got back home
Without a dime.

When I dropped that nickel
In a subway slot,
I wouldn't have dropped it,
Knowing what I got.

I could just as well've
Stayed home inside:
My bread wasn't buttered
On neither side.

LANGSTON HUGHES

A SAD SONG ABOUT
GREENWICH VILLAGE

She lives in a garret
    Up a haunted stair,
And even when she's frightened
    There's nobody to care.

She cooks so small a dinner
    She dines on the smell,
And even if she's hungry
    There's nobody to tell.

She sweeps her musty lodging
    As the dawn steals near,
And even when she's crying
    There's nobody to hear.

I haven't seen my neighbor
    Since a long time ago,
And even if she's dead
    There's nobody to know.

FRANCES PARK

FACES

People that I meet and pass
    In the city's broken roar,
Faces that I lose so soon
    And never found before,

Do you know how much you tell
    In the meeting of our eyes,
How ashamed I am, and sad
    To have pierced your poor disguise?

Secrets rushing without sound
    Crying from your hiding places—
Let me go, I cannot bear
    The sorrow of the passing faces.

—People in the restless street,
    Can it be, oh, can it be
In the meeting of our eyes
    That you know as much of me?

SARA TEASDALE

COULD BE

Could be Hastings Street,

Or Lenox Avenue.
Could be 18th and Vine
And still be true.

Could be 5th and Mound,
Could be Rampart:
When you pawned my watch
You pawned my heart.

Could be you love me
Could be that you don't.
Might be that you'll come back
Like as not you won't.

Hastings Street is weary,
Also Lenox Avenue.
Any place is dreary
Without my watch and you.

LANGSTON HUGHES

THE GREATEST CITY

What do you think endures?
Do you think the greatest city endures?
Or a teeming manufacturing state? or a prepared
    constitution? or the best built steamships?
Or hotels of granite and iron? or any chef-d'oeuvres
    of engineering, forts, armaments?
Away! These are not to be cherished for themselves,
They fill their hour, the dancers dance, the musicians
    play for them,
The show passes, all does well enough of course,
All does very well till one flash of defiance.

The greatest city is that which has the greatest men
    and women,
If it be a few ragged huts, it is still the greatest city
    in the whole world.

WALT WHITMAN

JAZZ FANTASIA

Drum on your drums, batter on your banjos,
sob on the long cool winding saxophones.
Go to it, O jazzmen.

Sling your knuckles on the bottom of the happy
tin pans, let your trombones ooze, and go husha-
husha-hush with the slippery sand-paper.

Moan like an autumn wind in the lonesome treetops, moan soft like you wanted somebody terrible,
cry like a racing car slipping away from a motorcycle
cop, bang-bang! you jazzmen, bang altogether drums,
traps, banjos, horns, tin cans—make two people fight
on the top of a stairway and scratch each other's
    eyes
in a clinch tumbling down the stairs.

Can the rough stuff . . . now a Mississippi steamboat
pushes up the night river with a hoo-hoo-hoo-oo . . .
and the green lanterns calling to the high soft stars
. . . a red moon rides on the humps of the low river
hills . . . go to it, O jazzmen.

CARL SANDBURG

CHILDHOOD

Can I forget—
The barren chalked garret
In which we huddled,
Curling from cold,
Fighting for the shifting coats?

Can I forget—
The stinking cellar
Where the sunshine was alien
And the orange crate bare?

Can I forget—
Mother, nursing the lame
Washing the ghetto dead—
For scanty crumbs?

I can't forget
When still trapped
On the hook of greed
Warding off the hurt
Of the desperate claws.

HENRI PERCIKOW

A Little Boy Stood
on the Corner

DECEMBER

A little boy stood on the corner
And shoveled bits of dirty, soggy snow
Into the sewer—
With a jagged piece of tin.

He was helping spring come.

SANDERSON VANDERBILT

TEN O'CLOCK

Our skipping ropes lie silent,
Our hop-scotch squares are dead,
And we are home at ten o'clock
    Tucked in bed.
We jumped away the morning,
We hopped away the noon,
We skipped away the evening;
    Night came soon.
Time looped up our skipping rope,
He blackened out our squares,
He took us by our trusting hands
    And led us to the stairs.

PATRICIA HUBBELL

FOOD

When I go walking down the street
There's lots of things I like to eat,

Like pretzels from the pretzel man
And buttered popcorn in a can,

And chocolate peppermint to lick
And candy apples on a stick.

Oh, there are many things to chew
While walking down the avenue.

MARCHETTE CHUTE

VERN

When walking in a tiny rain
Across the vacant lot,
A pup's a good companion—
If a pup you've got.

And when you've had a scold,
And no one loves you very,
And you cannot be merry,
A pup will let you look at him,
And even let you hold
His little wiggly warmness—

And let you snuggle down beside.
Nor mock the tears you have to hide.

GWENDOLYN BROOKS

FORTUNE

Fortune
has its cookies to give out

which is a good thing

since it's been a long time since

that summer in Brooklyn
when they closed off the street
one hot day
and the

FIREMEN

turned on their hoses

and all the kids ran out in it

in the middle of the street

and there were

maybe a couple dozen of us

out there

with the water squirting up

                    to the

                 sky

                       and all over
                            us

        there was maybe only six of us
                        kids altogether
            running around in our
                        barefeet and birthday
                suits
                and I remember Molly but then

        the firemen stopped squirting their hoses
                all of a sudden and went
                        back in
                their firehouse
                and
                started playing pinochle again
                        just as if nothing
                        had ever
                                happened
    while I remember Molly
                            looked at me and

        ran in

    because I guess really we were the only ones there

                    LAWRENCE FERLINGHETTI

                                            85

from **THE BALL POEM**

What is the boy now, who lost his ball,
What what is he to do? I saw it go
Merrily bouncing, down the street, and then
Merrily over—there it is in the water!
No use to say "O there are other balls":
An ultimate shaking grief fixes the boy
As he stands rigid, trembling, staring down
All his young days into the harbour where
His ball went. I would not intrude on him,
A dime, another ball, is worthless. . . .

JOHN BERRYMAN

KID IN THE PARK

Lonely little question mark
on a bench in the park:

See the people passing by?
See the airplanes in the sky?
See the birds
flying home
before
dark?

Home's just around
the corner
there—
but not really
anywhere.

LANGSTON HUGHES

Two girls of twelve or so at a table
in the Automat, smiling at each other
and the world; eating sedately.
And a tramp, wearing two or three tattered coats,
dark with dirt, mumbling, sat down beside them—
Miss Muffit's spider.
But, unlike her, they were not frightened away,
and did not shudder as they might if older and look
        askance.
They did steal a glance
at their dark companion and were slightly amused:
in their shining innocence seeing
in him only another human being.

CHARLES REZNIKOFF

ITALIAN EXTRAVAGANZA

Mrs. Lombardi's month-old son is dead,
I saw it in Rizzo's funeral parlor,
A small purplish wrinkled head.

They've just finished having high mass for it;
They're coming out now
. . . wow, such a small coffin!
And ten black cadillacs to haul it in.

GREGORY CORSO

THE CHILD ON THE CURBSTONE

The headlights raced; the moon, death-faced,
Stared down on that silver river.
I saw through the smoke the scarlet cloak
Of a boy who could not shiver.

His father's hand forced him to stand,
The traffic thundered slaughter;
One foot he thrust in the whirling dust
As it were running water.

As in a dream I saw the stream
Scatter in drops that glisten;
They flamed, they flashed, his brow they splashed,
And danger's son was christened.

The portent passed; his fate was cast,
Sea-farer, desert-ranger.
Tearless I smiled on that fearless child
Dipping his foot in Danger.

ELINOR WYLIE

TAUGHT ME PURPLE

My mother taught me purple
    Although she never wore it.
Wash-grey was her circle,
    The tenement her orbit.

My mother taught me golden
    And held me up to see it,
Above the broken molding,
    Beyond the filthy street.

My mother reached for beauty
    And for its lack she died,
Who knew so much of duty
    She could not teach me pride.

EVELYN TOOLEY HUNT

MOTHER TO SON

Well, son, I'll tell you:
Life for me ain't been no crystal stair.
It's had tacks in it,
And splinters,
And boards torn up,
And places with no carpet on the floor—
Bare.
But all the time
I'se been a-climbin' on,
And reachin' landin's,
And turnin' corners,
And sometimes goin' in the dark
Where there ain't been no light.
So, boy, don't you turn back.
Don't you set down on the steps
'Cause you find it kinder hard.
Don't you fall now—
For I'se still goin', honey,
I'se still climbin',
And life for me ain't been no crystal stair.

LANGSTON HUGHES

Like Bees in a Tunneled Hive

TALL CITY

Here houses rise so straight and tall
That I am not surprized at all
To see them simply walk away
Into the clouds—this misty day.

SUSAN NICHOLS PULSIFER

SQUARES AND ANGLES

Houses in a row, houses in a row,
Houses in a row.
Squares, squares, squares.
Houses in a row.
People already have square souls,
Ideas in a row,
And angles on their backs.
I myself shed a tear yesterday
Which was—good heavens——square.

ALFONSINA STORNI

(*Translated from the Spanish by Seymour Resnick*)

EVEN NUMBERS

I

A house like a man all lean and coughing,
a man with his two hands in the air at a cry,
"Hands up."
A house like a woman shrunken and stoop-
    shouldered,
shrunken and done with dishes and dances.
These two houses I saw going uphill in Cincinnati.

II

Two houses leaning against each other like drunken
brothers at a funeral,
Two houses facing each other like two blind
    wrestlers
hunting a hold on each other,
These four scrawny houses I saw on a dead level
cinder patch in Scranton, Pennsylvania.

III

And by the light of a white moon in Waukesha,
    Wisconsin,
I saw a lattice work in lilac time . . . white-mist
            lavender
. . . a sweet moonlit lavender . . .

CARL SANDBURG

RAT RIDDLES

There was a gray rat looked at me
with green eyes out of a rathole.

"Hello, rat," I said,
"Is there any chance for me
to get on to the language of the rats?"

And the green eyes blinked at me,
blinked from a gray rat's rathole.

"Come again," I said,
"Slip me a couple of riddles;
there must be riddles among the rats."

And the green eyes blinked at me
and a whisper came from the gray rathole:
"Who do you think you are and why is a rat?
Where did you sleep last night and why do you
       sneeze
   on Tuesdays? And why is the grave of a rat no
   deeper than the grave of a man?"

And the tail of a green-eyed rat
Whipped and was gone at a gray rathole.

CARL SANDBURG

freddy the rat perishes

listen to me there have
been some doings here since last
i wrote there has been a battle
behind that rusty typewriter cover
in the corner
you remember freddy the rat well
freddy is no more but
he died game the other
day a stranger with a lot of
legs came into our
little circle a tough looking kid
he was with a bad eye
who are you said a thousand legs
if i bite you once
said the stranger you won t ask
again he he little poison tongue said
the thousand legs who gave you hydrophobia
i got it by biting myself said
the stranger i m bad keep away
from me where i step a weed dies
if i was to walk on your forehead it would
raise measles and if
you give me any lip i ll do it
they mixed it then
and the thousand legs succumbed
well we found out this fellow

was a tarantula he had come up from
south america in a bunch of bananas
for days he bossed us life
was not worth living he would stand in
the middle of the floor and taunt
us ha ha he would say where i
step a weed dies do
you want any of my game i was
raised on red pepper and blood i am
so hot if you scratch me i will light
like a match you better
dodge me when i am feeling mean and
i don t feel any other way i was nursed
on a tabasco bottle if i was to slap
your wrist in kindness you
would boil over like job and heaven
help you if i get angry give me
room i feel a wicked spell coming on

last night he made a break at freddy
the rat keep your distance
little one said freddy i m not
feeling well myself somebody poisoned some
cheese for me i m as full of
death as a drug store i
feel that i am going to die anyhow
come on little torpedo come on don t stop
to visit and search then they
went at it and both are no more . . .
. . . . we dropped freddy

off the fire escape into the alley with
military honors
                    archy

                              DON MARQUIS

FLIGHT
for K.

Like a glum cricket
the refrigerator is singing
and just as I am convinced

that it is the only noise
in the building, a pot falls
in 2B. The neighbors on

both sides of me suddenly
realize that they have not
made love to their wives

since 1947. The racket
multiplies. The man down hall
is teaching his dog to fly.

The fish are disgusted
and beat their heads blue
against a cold aquarium. I too

lose control and consider
the dust huddled in the corner
a threat to my endurance.

Were you here, we would not
tolerate mongrels in the air,
nor the conspiracies of dust.

We would drive all night,
your head tilted on my shoulder.
At dawn, I would nudge you

with my anxious fingers and say,
Already we are in Idaho.

JAMES TATE

APARTMENT HOUSE

A filing-cabinet of human lives
Where people swarm like bees in tunneled hives,
Each to his own cell in the towered comb,
Identical and cramped—we call it home.

GERALD RAFTERY

CITY NUMBER

The soiled city oblongs stand sprawling,
The blocks and house numbers go miles.
Trucks howl rushing the early morning editions.
Night-club dancers have done their main floor show,
Tavern trios improvise "Show me the way to go
    home."
Soldiers and sailors look for street corners, house
    numbers.
Night watchmen figure halfway between midnight
    and breakfast.
Look out the window now late after the evening that
        was
    On a south sky of pigeon-egg blue
    Long clouds float in a silver moonbath.

CARL SANDBURG

FACTORY WINDOWS ARE ALWAYS BROKEN

Factory windows are always broken.
Somebody's always throwing bricks,
Somebody's always heaving cinders,
Playing ugly Yahoo tricks.

Factory windows are always broken.
Other windows are let alone.
No one throws through the chapel-window
The bitter, snarling, derisive stone.

Factory windows are always broken.
Something or other is going wrong.
Something is rotten—I think, in Denmark.
End of the factory-window song.

VACHEL LINDSAY

CONSTRUCTION

The house frames hang like spider webs
Dangling in the sun,
While up and down the wooden strands
The spider workers run.
They balance on the two-by-fours,
They creep across the beams,
While down below, the heap of wood,
A spider-stockpile, gleams.
The spider-workers spin the web
And tack it tight with nails.
They ready it against the night
    When all work ends.

PATRICIA HUBBELL

ON WATCHING THE
CONSTRUCTION
OF A SKYSCRAPER

Nothing sings from these orange trees,
Rindless steel as smooth as sapling skin,
Except a crane's brief wheeze
And all the muffled, clanking din
Of rivets nosing in like bees.

BURTON RAFFEL

The Park Is Green
and Quiet

The park is green and quiet
except for a bush
with as many white flowers as leaves
and the gardener—crooked leg, malicious eye—
tearing at the weeds.

Beneath the trees
strut robber knights
in black speckled armor:
I know them,
although they look like starlings.

CHARLES REZNIKOFF

A CITY PARK

Timidly
Against a background of brick tenements
Some trees spread their branches
Skyward.
They are thin and sapless,
They are bent and weary—
Tamed with captivity;
And they huddle behind the fence
Swaying helplessly before the wind,
Forward and backward
Like a group of panicky deer
Caught in a cage.

ALTER BRODY

CITY SPARROW

Who's that dusty stranger? What's he doing here?
That city-bred bird with the ill-bred leer?

Perching on branches like telegraph wires?
Chirping his slang above passionate fires?

Poking his head about, twitching his tail,
Getting drunk in our pools as if they were ale?

Never accepting, but stealing our rations?
Acting toward us as he would to relations?

Who asked him hither, what led him this way?
With his critical carping, his mockery, eh?

And worse than all these, he's a jerky reminder
Of winters, of towns, and of people no kinder.

ALFRED KREYMBORG

TRINITY PLACE

The pigeons that peck at the grass in Trinity
      Churchyard
        Are pompous as bankers. They walk with an air,
          they preen
Their prosperous feathers. They smugly regard
      their beauty
        They are plump, they are sleek. It is only the
          men who are lean.

The pigeons scan with disfavor the men who sit
      there,
        Listless in sun or shade. The pigeons sidle
Between the gravestones with shrewd, industrious
      motions.
        The pigeons are busy. It is only the men who are
          idle.

The pigeons sharpen their beaks on the stones, and
      they waddle
        In dignified search of their proper, their daily
          bread.
Their eyes are small with contempt for the men on
      the benches.
        It is only the men who are hungry. The pigeons
          are fed.

PHYLLIS McGINLEY

WATER PICTURE

In the pond in the park
all things are doubled:
Long buildings hang and
wriggle gently. Chimneys
are bent legs bouncing
on clouds below. A flag
wags like a fishhook
down there in the sky.

The arched stone bridge
is an eye, with underlid
in the water. In its lens
dip crinkled heads with hats
that don't fall off. Dogs go by,
barking on their backs.
A baby, taken to feed the
ducks, dangles upside-down,
a pink balloon for a buoy.

Treetops deploy a haze of
cherry bloom for roots,
where birds coast belly-up
in the glass bowl of a hill;
from its bottom a bunch
of peanut-munching children

is suspended by their
sneakers, waveringly.

A swan, with twin necks
forming the figure three,
steers between two dimpled
towers doubled. Fondly
hissing, she kisses herself,
and all the scene is troubled:
water-windows splinter,
tree-limbs tangle, the bridge
folds like a fan.

MAY SWENSON

CENTRAL PARK TOURNEY

Cars
In the Park
With long spear lights
Ride at each other
Like armored knights;
Rush,
Miss the mark,
Pierce the dark,
Dash by!
Another two
Try.

Staged
In the Park
From dusk
To dawn,
The tourney goes on:
Rush,
Miss the mark,
Pierce the dark,
Dash by!
Another two
Try.

MILDRED WESTON

Night Song

MANHATTAN LULLABY
(for Richard—one day old)

Now lighted windows climb the dark,
    The streets are dim with snow,
Like tireless beetles, amber-eyed,
    The creeping taxis go.
Cars roar through caverns made of steel,
    Shrill sounds the siren horn,
And people dance and die and wed—
    And boys like you are born.

RACHEL FIELD

The shopgirls leave their work
quietly.

Machines are still, tables and chairs
darken.

The silent rounds of mice and roaches begin.

CHARLES REZNIKOFF

The lightning bug has wings of gold;
The goldbug wings of flame;
The bedbug has no wings at all,
But it gets there just the same.

AUTHOR UNKNOWN

PRELUDE

The winter evening settles down
With smell of steaks in passageways.
Six o'clock.
The burnt-out ends of smoky days.
And now a gusty shower wraps
The grimy scraps
Of withered leaves about your feet
And newspapers from vacant lots;
The showers beat
On broken blinds and chimney-pots.
And at the corner of the street
A lonely cab-horse steams and stamps.
And then the lighting of the lamps.

T. S. ELIOT

NIGHT

from *The Windy City*

Night gathers itself into a ball of dark yarn.
Night loosens the ball and it spreads.
The lookouts from the shores of Lake Michigan
    find night follows day,
      and ping! ping! across sheet gray
      the boat lights put their signals.
Night lets the dark yarn unravel,
Night speaks and the yarns change
    to fog and blue strands.

CARL SANDBURG

THE FOG

I saw the fog grow thick,
    Which soon made blind my ken;
It made tall men of boys,
    And giants of tall men.

It clutched my throat;
    Nothing was in my head
Except two heavy eyes
    Like balls of burning lead.

And when it grew so black
    That I could know no place,
I lost all judgment then,
    Of distance and of space.

The street lamps, and the lights
    Upon the halted cars,
Could either be on earth
    Or be the heavenly stars.

A man passed by me close,
    I asked my way, he said,
'Come, follow me, my friend' —
    I followed where he led.

He rapped the stones in front,
　'Trust me,' he said, 'and come';
I followed like a child—
　A blind man led me home.

W. H. DAVIES

THE STREET

Here is a long and silent street.
I walk in blackness and I stumble and fall
and rise, and I walk blind, my feet
trampling the silent stones and the dry leaves.
Someone behind me also tramples, stones, leaves:
if I slow down, he slows;
if I run, he runs   I turn   :   nobody.
Everything dark and doorless,
only my steps aware of me,
I turning and turning among these corners
which lead forever to the street
where nobody waits for, nobody follows me,
where I pursue a man who stumbles
and rises and says when he sees me   :   nobody.

OCTAVIO PAZ

(Translated by Muriel Rukeyser)

ACQUAINTED WITH THE NIGHT

I have been one acquainted with the night.
I have walked out in rain—and back in rain.
I have outwalked the furthest city light.

I have looked down the saddest city lane.
I have passed by the watchman on his beat
And dropped my eyes, unwilling to explain.

I have stood still and stopped the sound of feet
When far away an interrupted cry
Came over houses from another street,

But not to call me back or say good-by;
And further still at an unearthly height,
One luminary clock against the sky

Proclaimed the time was neither wrong nor right.
I have been one acquainted with the night.

ROBERT FROST

STARS

O, sweep of stars over Harlem Streets,
O, little breath of oblivion that is night.
>   A city building
>   To a mother's song.
>   A city dreaming
>   To a lullaby.
Reach up your hand, dark boy, and take a star.
Out of the little breath of oblivion
>   That is night
>   Take just
>   One star.

LANGSTON HUGHES

from WHEN DAWN COMES TO THE CITY: NEW YORK

The tired cars go grumbling by,
    The moaning, groaning cars,
And the old milk carts go rumbling by
    Under the same dull stars.
Out of the tenements, cold as stone,
    Dark figures start for work;
I watch them sadly shuffle on,
    'Tis dawn, dawn in New York.

The tired cars go grumbling by,
    The crazy, lazy cars,
And the same milk carts go rumbling by
    Under the dying stars.
A lonely newsboy hurries by,
    Humming a recent ditty;
Red streaks through the gray of the sky,
    The dawn comes to the city.

CLAUDE McKAY

HARLEM NIGHT SONG

Come,
Let us roam the night together
Singing

I love you

Across
The Harlem roof-tops
Moon is shining.
Night sky is blue
Stars are great drops
Of golden dew.

Down the street
A band is playing.

I love you

Come,
Let us roam the night together
Singing.

LANGSTON HUGHES

Let Me Pry Loose Old Walls

ON THE EXPRESSWAY

The city rolls,
Block by block,
Backward through the cold.
I watch it pass.
Apartments of the rich blaze
And fade; mills
Smoulder into suburbs or slums;
And all's a fabric spun
From bleached grass,
And winter sun.

ROBERT DANA

OUR LARGEST AND SMALLEST CITIES

Large towns, small towns,
Vacant cities, busy cities,
sports coats, nightgowns,
laughs, cries, sighs, pities.

All these build our largest and smallest cities.
Candy bars, grocery stores
hold the hearts of our gay kiddies
and the gossip of our neighborhood biddies.

Loud cries, mumbled noises,
Teen-agers, small kids' voices,
Freedom-riders, Jackson Advocate subscribers,
neighborhood people, political bribers.

Large towns, small towns,
vacant cities, busy cities,
sports coats, nightgowns,
laughs, sighs, cries, pities,
All these build our largest and smallest cities.

NETTIE RHODES

TRANSCONTINENT

Where the cities end, the
dumps grow the oil-can shacks
from Portland, Maine,

to Seattle. Broken
cars rust in Troy, New York,
and Cleveland Heights.

On the train, the people
eat candy bars, and watch,
or fall asleep.

When they look outside and
see cars and shacks, they know
they're nearly there.

DONALD HALL

LIVING AMONG THE TOILERS

I live among workers
Where life ebbs in shadows
And see waning petals
In the depths of children's eyes.

I share the conveyor belt—
And feel the iron wheel
Ride my bones,
Crushing.

I hear the cry
Of the cheated
And add my fist,
Accusing.

My vision clear,
I sing
Of a chromed tomorrow
Held in my calloused palm.

HENRI PERCIKOW

IS GOD DEAD?

Is God dead?
He could be vacationing,
Or could He be selling flowers
    at the corner of Germantown and Penn?
Maybe He's visiting a shrink.
Or could He be in your living room,
    wagging His tail,
When you come home from a hard day's teaching?
Maybe He's in jail for starting a riot.
Or figuring a way to peace for a war He didn't start.
Where is God? Is God dead?

MARTIN RADCLIFFE

DREAM DEFERRED

What happens to a dream deferred?

Does it dry up
like a raisin in the sun?
Or fester like a sore—
And then run?
Does it stink like rotten meat?
Or crust and sugar over—
like a syrupy sweet?

Maybe it just sags
like a heavy load.

Or does it explode?

LANGSTON HUGHES

PRAYERS OF STEEL

Lay me on an anvil, O God.
Beat me and hammer me into a crowbar.
Let me pry loose old walls;
Let me lift and loosen old foundations.

Lay me on an anvil, O God.
Beat me and hammer me into a steel spike.
Drive me into the girders that hold a skyscraper to-
      gether.
Take red-hot rivets and fasten me into the central
      girders.
Let me be the great nail holding a skyscraper through
      blue nights into white stars.

CARL SANDBURG

Index of Poets and Titles

Index of First Lines

NANCY LARRICK was born in Winchester, Virginia, a small town in the rural Shenandoah Valley. At fifteen she entered Goucher College, then located in the heart of Baltimore, where streetcars and buses rattled past classrooms and residence halls. "That's when the city got into my blood," she says.

After teaching for a number of years in the public schools of Winchester, she returned to the city, this time to New York where she got her master's degree at Columbia University and her doctorate at New York University. For 15 years she was a New York editor, first of children's magazines and then of children's books. During this period—and on the night shift—she taught several classes of city teachers at the Bank Street College of Education and in the School of Education at NYU.

Dr. Larrick is now Adjunct Professor of Education at Lehigh University and director of the Lehigh Workshop in Poetry for Children. She is the author of *A Parent's Guide to Children's Reading, A Parent's Guide to Children's Education,* and *A Teacher's Guide to Children's Books,* as well as the editor of several anthologies of poetry for children and an album of poetry records for children.

In 1960 Nancy Larrick and her husband, Alexander L. Crosby, moved to Bucks County, Pennsylvania, where they have a 200-year-old stone farmhouse, 33 wooded acres—and always a book of Holland Tunnel tickets to speed their frequent trips back to Manhattan.

DATE DUE